SURVIVING TEXAS PROBATE

A Practical Guide to Surviving Dying in Texas

Texas Trust Law

Wills * Trusts * Probate * Asset Protection *

Special Needs Planning

Austin * San Antonio * Georgetown * Highland Lakes

www.TexasTrustLaw.com

The Peace of Mind People®

Table of Contents

Preface

The purpose of this handbook is to help explain the estate administration process in Texas by providing a checklist of the steps that generally must be taken. It will also show how to safeguard the financial interests of the immediate surviving family members following the death of a loved one. These instructions should prove helpful whether the deceased had meticulously planned, or whether there was no planning at all. Making the estate administration process less mysterious and, hopefully understandable, is our goal for this book.

Introduction

By Zachary Wiewel

Losing a loved one is one of the most difficult experiences in life. The loss can shake you to your very core, and you may experience a variety of emotions as a result, including deep sorrow and fear for the future. You may also become depressed, find that you are easily overwhelmed by the thought of having to accomplish even the smallest and most routine tasks, have trouble focusing, and feel like you are sometimes living in a fog. For example, some of our clients have told us that they ran red lights, left pots burning on the stove, and did other things that put them and those around them in potential danger because the death of their loved one left them feeling disoriented.

Coupling the stress of a loss with the legal work that needs to be done can be overwhelming. Whatever your emotional state, however, during the days, weeks, and even months ahead, you will have to make important decisions and undertake specific activities related to the deceased's estate, assuming that you are designated as the executor of the will, the trustee of a living trust, or that the probate court named you administrator of the estate if there was no estate plan.

Being an executor, administrator or trustee may sound slightly daunting given how you may be feeling right now. However, there are resources that can help you cope with your emotions so they do not impede your ability to handle your responsibilities. These include grief counselors, bereavement support groups, and your religious faith, not to mention your family members and friends. In addition, an estate and probate attorney who understands the unique anxiety that you face can provide you with invaluable assistance throughout the estate administration process and can also help you make sure that *you* have the appropriate estate plan in place.

We hope that you will also find this handbook, *Surviving Dying in Texas*, to be a very helpful resource because we wrote it with you in mind. For example, in simple language, this handbook:

- Distinguishes between a will and a living trust,

- Provides an overview of the estate administration process,

- Explains how the Texas probate process works,

- Alerts you to the information and documents you will need during that process,

- Prepares you to work effectively and efficiently with a Texas attorney and CPA,

- Educates you about the actions you should take right away as executor or trustee, and

- Warns you about the things you, or someone else (such as an adult child or a family friend) should never do immediately after a death without your attorney's advice.

The handbook also sets out our *Six Rules for Survival* for surviving spouses and provides basic advice about the kinds of estate planning you may need to do now.

Tip: This book assumes that you will be acting as the executor, administrator, or trustee of the deceased's estate. If someone other than you will have one or more of these roles, be sure to share this handbook with them.

Chapter One

Understanding the Texas Estate Administration Process

The deceased's estate assets, with some exceptions, must go through an administration process before they can be transferred to the proper recipients. What type of estate plan is in place will determine who receives the property. If there is no estate plan, or an inaccurate or an incomplete one, the deceased's legal heirs will inherit some or all. Legal heirs are the individuals related to the deceased that Texas law says are entitled to the assets. If there is a valid and complete will or living trust, the assets will pass according to the terms of those documents, and the details of the administration process will depend on the terms of those documents.

If you are the executor of the will, or the trustee of the living trust, you will be responsible, among other things, for beginning the administration process and for carrying out the wishes the deceased spelled out in the estate plan.

This chapter provides an overview of your duties and legal obligations. It also provides a brief explanation of what will happen if your loved one died without an estate plan.

> **Tip:** Before you can carry out your responsibilities as executor under the will, you must ask the probate court to formally appoint you to that position. You are NOT the executor until the court approves you and you take your oath. Many institutions require Letters Testamentary in order for you to conduct business on behalf of your loved one's estate, and these can only be obtained by order of the probate court.

> **Tip:** Although you may have been designated as the executor or trustee, you are not required to serve in that role if you don't want to, or if you don't feel emotionally equipped to take on any new responsibilities right now.

The Texas Estate Administration Process

If there is a WILL

As the executor of the will, you will need to:

- Initiate the probate process with the probate court in the appropriate Texas county;

- Comply with the rules of that process. Your activities will be supervised by the court in a "dependent" administration, unless the estate qualifies as for an "independent" administration;

- Locate and inventory all the assets in the estate;

- Identify the nature and amounts of any debts that were owed at the time of death, notify those creditors about the death so they can file claims with the probate court, and pay all the deceased's legitimate debts out of the assets in the estate (you must also pay all expenses associated with the probate of the estate and any taxes it may owe);

- Get the appropriate assets transferred to beneficiaries or to a testamentary trust established in the will (a testamentary trust is a kind of trust that does not come into existence until death, and the assets earmarked for it cannot be transferred to that trust until after the will is admitted to probate); and

- After all debts and expenses have been paid, transfer the title of the remaining assets out of the deceased's name and into the names of the people named in the will, once you have the authority from the court to do so.

Warning: Hopefully, the deceased maintained comprehensive records regarding the assets and debts. Otherwise, it will be up to you to gather all of the information you will need during the estate administration process, which can often be very challenging.

Warning: The probate process for many estates is simple and straightforward, but there are often problems. For example, a will may not be clearly worded, and *who* is entitled to *what* in the estate may be unclear. Also, someone may contest the validity of a will, or only a copy of a will may be able to be found. When there are problems such as these, the process can be more costly and time-consuming than normal.

Consult with a Texas estate and probate attorney before you even think about beginning any of the responsibilities as executor. Even though you may be named an executor, you are not the executor until the probate judge formally appoints you to that position and you take your oath. In fact, in Texas you MUST have a lawyer represent you in court; Texas is not a do-it-yourself state when it comes to probate. Among other things, your attorney will:

- Review the will,
- Tell you what to expect during the probate process,
- Alert you to any potential problems, and
- Answer your questions.

The type of estate administration process you will need to follow often depends on the type of assets in the estate, as well as the language of the will. Your attorney will let you know if you need to be bonded or if anything else needs to be done before you can carry out your responsibilities as executor.

> **Tip:** Texas has a probate process called a *Muniment of Title*. It differs from a standard probate because no executor is appointed and no inventory of assets is prepared. It can be helpful in limited circumstances, but normally a standard probate is recommended.

Chapter Four goes into much greater detail about all of the ways that an estate and probate attorney will help you during the estate administration process.

The Estate Administration Process

If there is a LIVING TRUST

Living trusts are popular substitutes for will planning. It is possible that the estate plan of the deceased includes a living trust. The ownership of the assets earmarked for the trust is usually transferred to it while the creator of the trust (the deceased) is alive. The legal term for transferring assets to a trust is *"funding the trust."* Once that has been accomplished, the trustee of the trust becomes the owner of those assets. The trustee controls the assets and distributes them according to the terms of the trust. A living trust is different from a will because trust administration usually occurs privately, without going to court.

As long as the deceased transferred all assets to the trust, those assets avoid the probate process. So, unlike an executor of a will, you are free to carry out your responsibilities as trustee of a trust with little or no court involvement. At a minimum, those responsibilities will include managing and transferring the trust assets according to the provisions of the living trust document.

> **Tip:** Probate is the court process required to remove the deceased's name from estate assets and to retitle those assets in the beneficiaries' names. A living trust can avoid probate when assets are titled in the name of a trust. Even though the trustmaker may pass away, the trust does not die; the trustee just administers the trust assets for the beneficiaries without court involvement.

> **Tip:** If any of the assets earmarked for the trust were not transferred to the trust before death, they may have to go through probate and will thus pass according to the will or by Texas intestacy law if there was no will. Normally, a "pour-over" will is created when there is a living trust, so that if any assets were mistakenly not put into the trust, the will can "pour" them into the trust by probating the will. The trust is the beneficiary of such a will, and the Executor can transfer the forgotten assets to the trust and then the trustee can get them to the trust beneficiaries.

Tip: A living trust is different from a testamentary trust because it is a legal entity that exists outside of a will, and because, as its name implies, it is created while someone is still living.

Warning: Even if the trust seems straight-forward, never attempt to act as trustee without consulting a qualified Texas estate and probate attorney. Trustees can create legal liability to themselves for even seemingly minor mistakes in administering the trust.

The Estate Administration Process

If there is NO ESTATE PLAN

If your loved one died without an estate plan – did not write a will and did not set up a living trust – there will likely be an heirship proceeding in probate court to determine who will inherit those assets according to Texas intestacy laws, or laws of inheritance. The people entitled to those assets are referred to as the legal heirs. There are two types of court administration proceedings when someone dies without a will or trust, a *Determination of Heirship* and a *Small Estate Affidavit*.

A Texas probate judge must determine who those legal heirs are. Most often, this is done through a *Determination of Heirship* proceeding. If there is a need for an estate representative to be appointed, the judge will appoint an administrator for the estate. An administrator's responsibilities will mirror those of an executor. The judge may require that the administrator post a bond before granting *Letters of Administration*, which are the same license to act on behalf of the estate for an administrator as the Letters Testamentary are for an executor under a will. Like a standard probate, the administration of an estate without a will can be "independent" or "dependent." All of the heirs must be over the age of 18 and must consent to an "independent" administration. Otherwise, a dependent administration is required and the administrator will be supervised by the court.

Determination of Heirship proceedings are often complex and involve at least two attorneys. One lawyer will represent the proposed administrator of the estate. The other attorney represents the deceased's unknown heirs and any heirs that are incapacitated. This second lawyer is called an *attorney ad litem* and is appointed by the Court. Unknown heirs are individuals whose names or locations are unknown. The attorney ad litem may discover such heirs during his or her investigation. Incapacitated heirs are heirs that are incapacitated by either being a minor, or an adult that, because of a physical or mental condition, is unable to provide for his or her own physical health or unable to manage his or her own financial affairs.

For very small estates with only a home and other assets of less than $75,000 (and no debt except the home mortgage), it may be possible to file a *Small Estate Affidavit*. This, like a Muniment of Title, involves no administration. A representative is not appointed by the Court, and property passes to the legal heirs simply by the judge's order approving the

Small Estate Affidavit. These can only be used in limited circumstances. The estate must be solvent, all of the heirs must be known and must sign the Small Estate Affidavit, and it only works to transfer title on real property if it was the deceased's homestead and all of the interest in the homestead is passing to someone that was living with the deceased before he or she died. The $75,000 cap on the estate size could change in the future.

There is an out of court method that is sometimes used regarding real estate when a person dies without a will. *Affidavits of Heirship* may be filed in the real property records. These affidavits set forth the marital and family history of the deceased, and Title Companies will often accept them in order to sell real property. If the *Affidavits of Heirship* sit uncontested in the real property records for five years, their validity is given similar weight to a Judgment Declaring Heirs according to the Texas Estates Code. A Texas estate planning and probate attorney can help determine if *Affidavits of Heirship* are a worthwhile alternative to a court process in your situation.

Your Legal Obligations During the Estate Administration Process

Regardless of your role in the process – executor, administrator, or trustee of a living trust – you will have some very important legal responsibilities during the estate administration process. For example, you will be expected to:

- Comply with the rules of the probate court as the executor or administrator of the estate (if you are the trustee of a living trust, you must carefully follow its terms);

- Carry out the directives spelled out in the will, living trust, and the law;

- Open a bank account in the name of the estate or trust (you may need an IRS Tax Identification Number, but your attorney or CPA will help you obtain this);

- Preserve the deceased's assets, (for example, you must insure and protect all of the assets);

- Act impartially (in other words, you cannot play favorites by doing anything that could benefit one of the beneficiaries or legal heirs at the expense of another);

- Avoid self-dealing (you cannot make decisions or take any actions that give you an advantage over another one of the beneficiaries);

- Provide full disclosure (keep all of the beneficiaries reasonably informed);

- Put the interests of other beneficiaries, if there are any, ahead of your own interests;

- Invest prudently (you should not put any of the estate's property in overly risky investments);

- Pay the appropriate bills as those become due;

- Maintain careful records regarding all of the assets and all expenses that are paid;

- File the appropriate tax returns; and

- Pay any taxes that may be due using the assets of the estate.

> **Warning:** Even if the estate does not owe any estate or inheritance taxes, you may want to file an estate death tax return. If you do, it generally must be filed no later than 9 months after the date of death, unless an extension is approved by the IRS. If any taxes are owed, those must be paid within nine months of the date of death.

Tip: Although you may not have to file an estate death tax return for the estate, it may be a very good idea for you to do so anyway. Why? There may be financial benefits by doing so. For example, you may establish the new date of death cost basis of assets owned by the deceased. That means that when those assets are sold after the death, you may owe substantially less in capital gains taxes. Also, if the deceased did not use all of his or her lifetime gift/estate exemption, filing the return will allow the surviving spouse to add the unused portion to their own lifetime exemption, which is another way that you can minimize or possibly even eliminate any taxes a surviving spouse might owe when he or she dies.

Tip: Some states (but not Texas) have their own estate and inheritance taxes, and you may owe these taxes even if you don't owe federal estate taxes. If the deceased owned property in one of those states, taxes may be owned there.

Warning: Not living up to your legal responsibilities during the estate administration process can have
VERY SEVERE consequences.

Chapter Two

What to Do Immediately After the Death of Your Loved One

Like many people who have lost a loved one, you may be unsure about what actions to take right away in regards to financial and legal affairs. Although your estate and probate attorney will provide you with more detailed information and instructions based on the specifics of the estate, Chapter Two and Chapter Three provide general guidelines for what you *should do* immediately, and equally important, will tell you what you (or anyone acting on behalf of the estate) *should not do* without your attorney's advice.

<u>*DO*</u>

- Read the will or living trust immediately, assuming there is one. It may spell out any wishes regarding funeral arrangements, desires for a memorial service, and other things you will need to act on right away. Also, look for an "Appointment for Disposition of Remains" which is a special Texas document that sets out who can legally make funeral arrangements and what sort of plans the deceased may have had, such as burial or cremation.

- If neither the spouse nor any of the estate's beneficiaries are living in the home of the deceased, remove and carefully store all valuables from the residence and consider changing the locks and turning off the utilities. You may also want to hire domestic help, security guards, and so forth the help maintain and protect the home.

- Maintain property and casualty insurance coverage on any personal property, automobiles, and real estate, including any items in storage. In addition, if no one is living in the home, find out if the liability insurance on it covers a vacant dwelling. If it does not, promptly consult with an insurance agent about changing the policy to reflect the fact that the house is empty.

- Determine any immediate cash needs and identify all accounts with ready cash. Also, determine if there are any expenses that need to be paid right away.

- Contact anyone who may owe money to the deceased and arrange for the payments to continue.

- Pull together all of the life and accident insurance policies.

- Locate any recent company retirement benefit statements,

- Try to locate the passwords for any accounts that may have been managed online, such as credit cards, charge cards, bank accounts, and investment accounts.

- Notify the Social Security Administration about the death of your loved one and return any Social Security payments he or she may receive in the future. Also, if you are the surviving spouse, or if there are any minor children, find out if you are entitled to Social Security survivor's benefits by calling 1-800-772-1213 to request an appointment at your local Social Security office; you cannot apply for the benefits online. If someone is eligible, the amount of the benefit will depend in part on the deceased's earnings record. For complete information about survivor's benefits, go to http://www.ssa.gov/survivorplan.

- If the deceased was a veteran, contact the U.S. Veteran's Administration (VA) office in your area or the national office right away. Under certain circumstances, the deceased's survivors may be eligible for a burial allowance. You should make all arrangements for these benefits through a funeral home, but more information is available at the U. S. Department of Veterans Affairs website, http://www.cem.va.gov/burial_benefits/index.asp. It is also possible that if you are the surviving spouse of a veteran, you (or your children) may be eligible for other VA benefits. For eligibility information and more, go to http://www.va.gov/opa/persona/dependent_survivor.asp or call 1-800-827-1000. Veterans are entitled to all of the following for free:

- o A gravesite for his or her casketed or cremated remains in one of the nation's national cemeteries (assuming there is space available);

- o Perpetual care;

- o A government headstone or marker; and

- o A burial flag.

- Contact the deceased's former employers as well as any labor unions or fraternal organizations they may have belonged to learn if you or someone else is entitled to any benefits. They might include life insurance death benefits, deferred compensation payments, stock, stock options, income from a pension, medical insurance, and so on.

> **Tip:** Unless there is a surviving spouse, the executor or administrator, or the trustee of a living trust should

cancel any credit cards, health insurance, long term care insurance, Medicare supplemental insurance, drug insurance, and magazine or other subscriptions and ask for appropriate refunds. They should find out how to access any potential benefits and if any of the accounts will pay a life insurance benefit, especially if the cause of death was an accident.

Tip: There may be life insurance through a credit card, travel club, alumni association, trade association or some other membership organization.

Tip: If you are eligible for survivor's benefits from Social Security because of the death of your spouse, you can receive reduced benefits starting at age 60, and if you are 50 and disabled, you can begin receiving benefits if your disability began within seven years of your spouse's death. If you are caring for a disabled child from your marriage who is younger than 16, you can receive survivor's benefits, no matter what your age.

Warning: You may have a very short time frame to exercise any stock options. If you miss the deadline, those will be lost. Be sure and make the estate and probate attorney aware of any stock options.

Warning: Taking any of the actions we advise against in Chapter Three could have lasting negative consequences for the estate. Furthermore, you could be held liable for any problems you may have created as a result.

Chapter Three

What Not to Do Immediately After the Death of Your Loved One

Many people want to do something – anything – right after the funeral to "get things going." Chapter Two told you the things you can do to move forward. This Chapter tells you what <u>NOT</u> to do without an estate and probate lawyer's explicit approval.

DON'T

- Do not use the deceased's powers of attorney because in Texas those become invalid at death.

- Do not give away or sell any of the deceased's assets. First, meet with an estate and probate attorney, and follow their advice carefully.

- Do not transfer any assets with beneficiary designations (such as the money in an IRA, 401k, payable-on-death (POD) account, transfer-on-death (TOD) account, annuity, or in joint tenancy with right to survivorship with another person) to the beneficiary for these assets until you have consulted with your estate and probate attorney, even though they may be accessible immediately after death. The same advice holds true for the assets in any living trust.

- Do not purchase any annuities using assets in the estate unless your attorney gives you written approval to do so.

> **Warning:** IRAs, retirement accounts and annuities may make up a substantial part of the estate, but those can create numerous problems if not handled appropriately. Therefore, we strongly advise that you consult with your estate and probate lawyer before you sign any paperwork related to these assets.

- Do not use the deceased's ATM, credit or debit cards unless you are already on the account.

- Do not tell any of the companies associated with the deceased's digital accounts about the death until you have discussed this with your attorney. By the same token, do not use any of the deceased's digital records, passwords or accounts without consulting with your attorney.

- Do not remove anything from any bank safe deposit box without a bank employee being present to help inventory the contents, even if you have regular access to the box. Only once you have a complete list of the safe deposit box contents, witnessed by the bank employee, should anything be removed.

- Do not "roll over" a retirement account without first talking with your attorney. This advice holds true *even if* your financial advisor tells you to roll it over right away. A rollover that is not timed correctly can have a negative financial impact on the surviving spouse.

- Do not ignore federal minimum distribution requirements for a retirement plan if the deceased was at least 70-1/2 when he or she died. Federal law says that every year, a certain amount of money must be withdrawn from a retirement plan once someone reaches that age, and the failure to do so will result in a stiff 50% penalty. Therefore, if your loved one was at least 70-1/2 and had not already taken the required minimum distribution in the year of death, that distribution must be taken that year. Otherwise, penalties will apply.

Chapter Four

Working with an Estate and Probate Attorney

Even though you may have never worked with a lawyer before, it is a *very* good idea to meet with an estate and probate attorney as soon as possible after the death of your loved one. This chapter prepares you to work with one by reviewing the many ways that attorney will help you, and it also explains how you may be charged for those services.

What to Expect From Your Attorney

At the start of the estate administration process, your attorney will review the estate plan, if any, and describe the steps necessary to begin evaluating the nature and value of the assets in the estate. If there is no estate plan, your attorney will explain what will happen as a result. As necessary, your attorney will also help you:

- Obtain the legal authority you need to act on behalf of the estate (probate the will, for example);

- Understand your legal obligations;

- Identify and inventory the assets;

- Determine any debts and other liabilities;

- Collect all legal and financial documents;

- Fill out the necessary paperwork;

- Work with a CPA to complete all tax returns that may have to be filed;

- Prepare any documents necessary to properly transfer the assets;

- Ensure that all of your decisions during the estate administration process are wise and legally defensible should anyone question something you have done; and

- Resolve any problems that may arise.

You can also expect to work with your attorney's legal assistants and other staff members. They can help you gather the information and documents you need and answer any non-legal questions you may have.

What to Bring to Your First Attorney Meeting

Your attorney will need very specific information about the deceased. Many will use an estate administration questionnaire that you fill out initially, but your attorney will also need:

- The will (if there is one);

- The living trust document (if one was prepared);

- Account statements (if you have them);

- Any prenuptial agreement that may be in effect;

- Any marriage license;

- Any prior divorce decrees;

- Adoption papers (if the deceased adopted any children, their adoption papers may be needed);

- Military discharge papers, (you will need these to access any benefits from the U.S. Department of Veterans Affairs, assuming he or she was a veteran);

- The deceased's Social Security number (you will have to provide this number many times throughout the estate administration process); and

- The deceased's death certificate (you will need this to get his or her assets transferred, even if the transfers will happen outside the probate process).

> **Tip:** Each asset transfer usually requires a separate certified death certificate. Because of this, we usually advise our clients to get at least 20 originals of them.

Although the funeral home you work with will provide you with some death certificates, you can obtain more from your local government.

In addition, your attorney will need to know if any of the deceased's beneficiaries:

- Have guardians or conservators. If they do, your attorney will want those names and addresses. Also, if any of the assets will be distributed in trust to the beneficiaries, your attorney will need the trustee's name and address.

- Are minors. If they are, your attorney will want their birth dates.

- Are deceased. Your attorney will need the dates of death for any beneficiaries that have already died and the names of their children, if any.

Tip: When you call to schedule your initial meeting with the attorney, ask about the documents you should bring to that meeting.

At some point during the estate administration process, you may also need:

- The deeds to all of the deceased's real estate, the most recent property tax statements for that property, and any appraisals for the real estate that were completed during the two years prior to the death;

- The titles to any automobiles, water craft, or recreational vehicles;

- Any personal checkbooks and check registers for the past five years;

- Any insurance policies, including life, auto, and home;

- Any annuity policies owned;

- Any contracts to which the deceased was a party, including leases, promissory notes and business agreements, like partnership agreements;

- Any bank accounts, investment statements, and so forth;

- Any retirement plans such as IRAs or 401ks, as well as the beneficiaries for the plans;

- Loan documents for assets the deceased owned at the time of death;

- Any mortgage statements for all outstanding real estate loans;

- Income tax returns for the past five years;

- All federal gift-tax returns (Form 709) the deceased may have filed;

- All federal estate tax returns (Form 706) the deceased may have filed on behalf of a spouse;

- Leases for any property owned by the deceased that were in effect at the time of death;

- Credit card statements;

- Information about any valuable personal property, like jewelry, wine, fine art, firearms, a stamp or coin collection, and so forth;

- The title to any burial plot or prepaid funeral plan;

- Stock option grants;

- Documents relating to any trust the deceased created;

- Any debts owed at death; and

- Any "Buy-Sell" agreements with the deceased's business partners.

How You Will Be Charged for Your Attorney's Services

Administering the estate of a deceased loved one can be an expensive process. In addition to potential attorneys' fees, there are court costs, accounting fees, and possibly a need for appraisals of real estate property and other assets. Some states such as California and Florida have certain laws that set out how much a lawyer is to be paid to probate a Will. In other states, such as Texas, the fees are not defined in the law. One survey of four states, including Texas, showed the average cost of probate can run two to three percent of the estate, which in our experience is high in most cases, but not all. Attorneys who work in this area of the law charge either flat fees (sometimes based on a percentage of the estate being administered) or fees based on an hourly rate. Lawyers billing hourly typically send invoices showing all the work the law firm has done for the estate, but clients often do not like paying for every phone call, fax, e-mail and copy. With a flat fee, the amount is clearly stated and does not create the sense of "nickel-and-diming" that hourly billing involves.

Living Trust administration also typically requires legal work. Often a trust administration can be less expensive than a probate, depending on the planning that was done. If all the assets are in the name of the trust, a formal court probate may be avoided. However, that just means the family escaped going to court. It does not mean that there is no legal work to be performed. The real difference is that with a living trust, the estate plan can be kept completely private and the work that needs to be done is scheduled for the family's convenience, not the judge's. Having no planning is the absolutely MOST expensive option, and typically involves multiple attorneys charging multiple amounts.

It is important to remember that there are fees involved with incapacity issues too. Those should be less with a Living Trust than if the incapacitated person only had a power of attorney. However, where there is no incapacity planning (living trust or power of attorney), the incapacitated person will almost always become the subject of a court supervised guardianship which is the absolutely MOST expensive option.

Chapter Five

All of the Assets May Not Be Treated Equally

(Probate vs. Non-Probate Property)

As we discussed, some of the deceased's assets may have to go through the probate process before they can be transferred to the deceased's beneficiaries, while others may transfer automatically. What will happen to a particular asset is generally determined by how it is titled or classified. This chapter provides you with an overview of which kinds of assets fall into which category.

What *Must* Go Through the Probate Process

Assets that must go through probate generally include:

- Those that are titled in the deceased's name only.

- Assets that the deceased owned with you (or someone else) as a tenant in common. When an asset is titled this way, the deceased was legally entitled to transfer his or her share of the asset to whomever they wanted, and that person may or may not have been the other owner(s).

- If the deceased was married and had lived in a community property state, the deceased's share often equals one-half the value of the property. Generally, any assets that you may have accumulated together or separately during your marriage while you were living in a community property state are classified as community property, with the exception of gifts or inheritances either of you may have received during that time. Texas, Arizona, California, Idaho, Louisiana, Nevada, Washington, New Mexico and Wisconsin are community property states. Also, in a handful of other states some assets acquired during a marriage may be treated as community property.

> **Tip:** Talk to your attorney if you want to *disclaim* or turn down any of the assets that were left to you. You may want to do this because you have no need for a particular asset or because you do not want the asset to increase the value of your taxable estate. When you disclaim an asset, the law determines who that asset will pass to. Other beneficiaries of the estate can also disclaim assets.

Warning: You must "disclaim" within nine months of the death.

Assets That *Do Not* Go Through the Probate Process

Some assets automatically transfer to someone else without probate. These include:

- <u>Joint tenancy with right of survivorship.</u> If any of the deceased's assets are titled this way, his or her share of those assets transfer to the other owner at death without any additional legal steps.

    Tip: Texas does not recognize Tenants-by-the-entirety, which is a form of ownership, where certain assets transfer automatically to the surviving spouse when the first spouse dies.

    Warning: If the deceased did not designate a beneficiary for certain accounts, or if the designated beneficiary has already died, the beneficiary may be the estate by default, which means that it will have to go through the probate process before the money associated with it can be distributed.

- Assets that were in a living trust. The terms of the trust determine to whom those are transferred.

- Beneficiary accounts. These include life insurance policies, IRAs, annuities, company retirement plans, transfer-on-death accounts (TOD) and payable-on-death (POD) accounts. If the deceased owned any of these assets, they had the right to designate a beneficiary – the person who would automatically receive the benefit from property after death. For example, if you are the beneficiary of someone's life insurance policy, you are immediately entitled to the policy proceeds, and if you are the beneficiary of the deceased's IRA, you are automatically entitled to whatever money is left in that account. If for any reason a beneficiary designation fails, the "default" beneficiary may end up being the "estate." If this happens, then a probate is required.

> **Warning:** If there are no clear instructions regarding what should happen to the personal property, (books, photographs, jewelry, knickknacks, family heirlooms, etc.) the family may become very divided over who should get what. This is because "the small stuff" can often be emotionally significant to the family members of someone who has died. When it is not

clear who that "stuff" should go to, feelings can get hurt, and old rivalries and jealousies can resurface. Consult with an estate and probate attorney before any personal property gets distributed. You and your attorney can discuss potential problems, and how to minimize the potential for discord.

Chapter Six

Time to Look at Your Own Estate Plan

It is extremely important, now that you have experienced a death, for you and your estate and probate attorney to review your own estate plan. Make this a top priority! There may be parts of your plan that absolutely need to change, and there may also be aspects of the plan that you *want* to change at this stage in your life.

To get you thinking, this chapter provides an overview of what you may need to do and highlights optional changes you may want to consider. Please note, however, that there is no one-size-fits-all estate plan because everyone's situation, goals and needs are different. Your attorney will help ensure that your plan is right for you.

Take a Look at Your Plan

We understand that estate planning may be the last thing you want to think about right now. However, it is important that you become totally familiar with your plan and that it reflects your wishes and meets your needs, especially after suffering the loss of a close loved-one.

Here are some examples of the kinds of things you may need to do in regard to your estate plan:

- Designate new beneficiaries if the deceased was your beneficiary,

- Name someone else as the executor of your will or the trustee of your trust if you had chosen the deceased for those roles,

- Reevaluate the terms of your will or living trust, and

- Take steps to minimize the amount of taxes your estate may owe when you die.

- Prepare a letter of instruction for your survivors. In the letter you can spell out your funeral/burial wishes, indicate the location of your important documents as well as the location of the keys to your safety deposit box, and explain how to find your computer passwords, among other things. At a minimum, make sure that your executor and/or trustee have a copy of the letter and know where the original is stored.

- Prepare a new financial power of attorney for your finances if the deceased was your financial agent. The new person you designate as your agent will manage your financial affairs if you become mentally incapacitated.

- Prepare a new medical power of attorney if your current document lists your deceased loved one as your health care agent (so that someone else can make health care decisions for you in the event of your incapacity).

And of course, if you <u>do</u> <u>not</u> have any type of estate plan, prepare one! At a minimum, it should include a will or a living trust, a durable power of attorney for your finances, and health care directives – a medical power of attorney, a living will (to terminate life support at the appropriate time), and a HIPAA Release so your doctors can talk with your family about your medical condition. Your estate and probate attorney will help you create the appropriate plan for you.

> **Tip:** It is very important that, in addition to reviewing your estate plan (or preparing one for the first time), you become totally familiar with your

finances, especially if you did not previously manage them. Schedule a meeting with your family's financial advisor and/or your CPA. Failing to become actively involved in the management of your money could cause your finances to take a big hit or conversely, cause you to miss out on a great opportunity to increase your wealth.

Warning: Tax laws change regularly, and your estate plan might have been affected by those.

Appendix I

Six *Rules of Survival* for Surviving Spouses

When you lose your spouse, you may be tempted to do things that you think will make you feel better, at least for a little while – sell your home or take a trip around the world, for example. Also, some of your family members or close friends may urge you to make big changes in your life. However, we are going to give you the exact same advice we give all of our clients who are in your situation: ***DON'T!*** Do not make any major decisions or changes right away. You may come to regret them, and they may have negative and long lasting consequences for your life. Give yourself time to gain some perspective about your loss. Then start thinking about what you want to do differently, if anything.

To help you avoid doing something in the immediate months ahead that you may regret later, here are our "Rules of Survival" for surviving spouses. Following these should make it easier for you to heal emotionally so that you can move forward with the rest of your life.

RULES FOR SURVIVING SPOUSES

Rule #1

- Do not make any major discretionary expenditures for a year. Certainly, there may be some big ticket items you have to spend money on – a new roof for your home for example. Otherwise, delay spending money on all major non-essentials for twelve months.

Rule #2

- Stay in your current home as long as it is practical. Give yourself plenty of time to figure out where you want to live – there or somewhere else. The decision you make today about where you will live could be very different from the decision you might make a year from now. Staying in your current home where you are surrounded by familiar things may be comforting at this stage in your life, and it may even make it easier for you to cope with your loss. Following our advice is especially important if the real estate market in your area is currently depressed. Waiting to sell until the market improves could mean that you net significantly more from a sale.

Rule #3

- Take care of yourself. For example, get a physical if you haven't had one recently, join a gym, go for walks, spend time with friends, take a class, meditate, and so forth. Staying healthy and active will help ease the sadness you are feeling and help alleviate any stress you may be experiencing due to your loss. Remind yourself that although you have suffered a major loss, your life is not over. You are where countless other people before you have been – starting a new phase in your life.

Rule #4

- Regardless of the size of the estate, close family members, relatives with whom you rarely communicate, and even long lost friends may ask you for financial help, possibly because they view what you have inherited as "found money." They may even try to pressure you into sharing your money or investing with them. However, do not lend any money, give away any money, or make any promises to do so in the future. There will be plenty of time for generosity later, assuming that you can afford to be generous with your money.

Rule #5

- If you are having a difficult time coping with your loss, talk with a trained and licensed grief counselor or therapist and consider joining a bereavement support group. Many churches and synagogues have these groups. You may find it healing to share your feelings with other people who are in your same situation.

Rule #6

- Connect with God. If your life seems lonely, fragile and maybe even frightening because of the loss you have experienced, spiritual counseling and fellowship can be extremely helpful.

Appendix II

Spiritual Support

A Prayer for Those Who Live Alone

I live alone, Lord, and I need your help as I struggle with my daily life.
I am often lonely and my home sometimes seems empty.

Please be my friend and comforter, dear Lord,
and help me seek companionship in you and your word.

Please keep me healthy, physically and, most importantly, mentally as I cope with
my loss.
I sometimes feel confused; help me to focus.

Please keep me safe from people who may want to take advantage of me,
and provide me with friends that are trustworthy and loyal.

Please help me not to fear the future.
Although I know that you own everything in the world, I sometimes worry about
money;
provide for me daily and increase my faith in You.

Please help me to look outside myself for people that I can serve
and with whom I can share my time and talents.

Finally, Lord, please help me to be a comfort to others who have suffered loss too;

make me a comforter of the afflicted and a source of hope and grace for them.

Thank you for all you provide both in this life and the next.

AMEN

Psalm 23

The Lord is my Shepherd, I shall not want;

He makes me lie down in green pastures,

He leads me beside quiet waters, He refreshes my soul.

' He guides me along the right paths for His name sake.

Even though I walk through the valley of the shadow of death, I will fear no

evil;

Your rod and your staff comfort me.

You prepare a table for me in the presence of my enemies.

You anoint my head with oil; my cup overflows.

Surely goodness and love will follow me all the days of my life,

And I will dwell in the house of the Lord forever.

Glossary of Common Legal Terms

This glossary defines many of the words and phrases you are apt to encounter during the estate administration process. It also tells you the meaning of words and phrases you are likely to come across when you review or create your own estate plan.

ADMINISTRATION
The process by which assets in the name of the deceased are legally transferred to his or her rightful heirs or beneficiaries. This can be accomplished through a will or a living trust.

ADVANCE HEALTH CARE DIRECTIVE or ADVANCE DIRECTIVES
In Texas, these terms refer to a Medical Power of Attorney and/or a Living Will. See the definition of those below

BENEFICIARY
A person who is (or will be) a recipient of benefits from a will, insurance policy, annuity, retirement account, estate or trust.

BEQUEST
A gift of property made in a will or trust.

BOND

An insurance policy that insures that a fiduciary will faithfully perform his or her duties relative to the deceased's estate. The executor, the administrator, and the trustee are all fiduciaries.

COMMUNITY PROPERTY

Most of the property acquired by a couple during their marriage while they resided in a community property state. Community property states are: Texas, Arizona, California, Idaho, Louisiana, New Mexico, Nevada, Washington, Wisconsin (and a handful of other states but only in very limited situations).

CONSERVATOR

In Texas this procedure is referred to as a Guardianship, and please see *Guardian* below.

DEATH TAX

Please see *Estate Tax* below.

DECEDENT

A person who has died.

DOD

A common abbreviation for Date of Death.

ESTATE

A legal entity that consists of all of someone's property and all the rights and responsibilities relating to them. This term is usually used in the context of the assets of someone after their death. A personal representative (an Executor or Administrator in probate, Trustee in a Trust) administers the property of a person after death. For Estate Tax purposes, the estate consists of everything a person owns or controls anywhere on Earth at the time of death.

ESTATE TAX

Sometimes used synonymously with the federal estate tax or death tax. Generically, this is any tax that is levied upon an estate as a whole which exceeds the allowable deduction. For married couples, the tax usually is not levied until the second death. Texas has NO state estate or inheritance tax.

EXECUTOR

An executor is someone named by the deceased in a Will and appointed by the probate court to administer that estate. The executor is under the ultimate authority of the probate court and can be removed if necessary. It is important to understand that an executor named in the will is NOT the executor of the estate until the probate court makes a formal appointment. Until then, the named executor has no power or control of the estate or its assets. An Administrator serves in a similar role as an Executor when the deceased died without a Will.

FIDUCIARY

A person (or corporation) who is in a position of trust and accountability, such as an executor, administrator, trustee, and so on.

GUARDIAN

There are two types of Guardians in Texas. The Guardian of the Estate is a person selected by the probate court to manage and distribute the assets of an incapacitated person. The Guardian of the Person is a person selected by the probate court to manage the health care of an incapacitated person.

HEIR

A person who is legally entitled to inherit property from a person who dies *intestate*, or without a will, according to the law of the state where the deceased resided or the property is located.

INHERITANCE TAX

Any death tax levied by a state government as opposed to the federal government. Not all states impose inheritance taxes. Texas has NO state estate or inheritance tax.

INTESTATE

The legal term that applies when someone dies without a valid will or living trust. It also applies when a will does not provide for the transfer of all of the deceased's property. When someone dies intestate he or she has forfeited all rights to determine who will receive the assets. That will be determined by the Law of Descent and Distribution in his or her state. In addition, the family of the deceased will almost always pay substantially higher attorney's fees and possibly higher estate taxes.

INVENTORY

A formal list of the assets of the deceased that often must be prepared and signed by the executor or administrator of an estate for the probate court.

JOINT TENANCY WITH RIGHT OF SURVIVORSHIP

A form of ownership of property among more than one person. When an owner dies, that person's interest transfers without any further legal action to the survivor, who then owns the entire asset.

LAW OF DESCENT AND DISTRIBUTION

A state statute that prescribes how the property of someone who dies without a will (*intestate*) will be distributed among his or her legal heirs.

LIVING TRUST

A trust created while you are alive. A Living Trust can be used to hold assets during a person's lifetime and thereby remove those assets from probate at the person's death. It is also sometimes called a "revocable living trust" because the terms of the trust can be changed by the creators of it. It is also known as an Inter Vivos Trust which means that it is created while someone is alive, as opposed to a "testamentary trust" which is a trust created by a Will.

LIVING WILL

This document states under what circumstances you want to discontinue life support.

PER STIRPES

Whenever a distribution is to be made to a person's descendants *per stirpes*, the distribution shall be divided into as many shares as there are then living children and deceased children of such person. Each then living child receives one share and the share of each deceased child is divided among that person's then living descendants in the same manner.

PERSONAL PROPERTY

There are two kinds personal property: *Tangible* property, which is anything that is moveable and can be touched, like a vehicle, home, furniture, etc., and *intangible* property or financial assets like cash, bank accounts, stocks, bonds, insurance, etc. Please see *Real Property*.

PERSONAL REPRESENTATIVE

A person or institution named in a will (the executor) or appointed by the probate court if there is no will (an administrator) to manage the estate of a deceased person. The term may also refer to a trustee and an agent under a durable power of attorney.

P.O.D.

An instruction to a depository institution such as a bank to pay the funds in the account to the beneficiary named by the account owner.

POUR-OVER WILL

A will which names a living trust as its principal beneficiary. Its function is to transfer or "pour over" into the trust any assets that were not already be in the trust at the time that the maker of the trust dies. The executor of the Pour-Over Will is responsible for transferring those assets to the trust at the end of the probate process.

PROBATE

The process of administering the estate of a deceased person under a probate court's jurisdiction. At the conclusion of the process, the deceased's beneficiaries (or legal heirs if there is no will) are identified, the debts and taxes are paid, and the assets that remain are distributed to the beneficiaries or heirs who are entitled to them.

REAL PROPERTY

Land and anything permanently attached to it, such as a home or some other kind of building.

REQUIRED BEGINNING DATE (RBD)

The date on which a retirement plan participant must begin taking at least minimum withdrawals from his or her retirement plan(s). This date is April 1st in the year following the year the participant reaches age 70-1/2.

REQUIRED MINIMUM DISTRIBUTIONS (RMD)

The withdrawals that a participant in a retirement plan is legally required to begin taking from the plan. In retirement planning, a participant is required to begin making withdrawals from retirement plans in the year after the Required Beginning Date. For those who inherit a retirement plan, required minimum distributions must begin by December 31 of the year following the death. These withdrawals must meet certain minimum distribution requirements, usually based on the payout election the participant makes at that time. In general, the participant must withdraw the funds over his or her life expectancy (but may do so more rapidly).

RESIDUARY ESTATE

The clause in a will or a living trust that disposes of all of the property of a deceased person that has not been previously mentioned in the document. This clause often begins, "All the rest, residue and remainder of my property, of whatsoever kind and nature, and wherever situated, I give to . . . "

REVOCABLE LIVING TRUST

Please see *Living Trust.*

ROLLOVER

Please see *Spousal Rollover.*

SEPARATE PROPERTY

The money someone earns while residing in a *common law state* or property owned prior to marriage in a *community property state*, as well as the assets that he or she acquires with those funds. In common law states as well as in most community property states, the property received by someone as a result of an inheritance, gift or personal injury settlement or award is also considered to be separate property.

SPOUSAL ROLLOVER

Where retirement plans and IRAs are payable to a surviving spouse, he or she has an option to *roll over* (or move) the funds in a plan or IRA into his or her own IRA. By doing so, the survivor is able to defer the income taxes on the funds.

SURVIVOR

A word that usually refers to the surviving spouse in a marriage.

TENANTS IN COMMON

A form of ownership in which two or more persons own undivided interests in property and each owner has rights to use the property. Unlike Joint Tenancy with Right of Survivorship, on the death of an owner, his or her share goes to that person's heirs or beneficiaries.

TESTAMENT

Another term for a will.

TESTAMENTARY TRUST

A trust created in a will. Once the will goes through the probate process, the appropriate assets are transferred to the trust.

TESTATOR

The legal term for someone who signs a will

T.O.D.

Transfer on death. A legal instrument attached to an ownership document of non-cash personal property, such as a car title or stock account, which changes title of the property to the beneficiary at the death of the owner.

TRUST

An agreement between a trustmaker (the person who sets up a trust) and his or her trustee, which gives the trustee the right to control the property the trustmaker transfers to the trust for the benefit of one or more beneficiaries. The trust agreement is a "rule book" which defines the trustee's powers and duties. In a living trust, the trustmaker is also the beneficiary and the trustee.

TRUSTEE

A person (or corporation) appointed by a trustmaker to control and manage the trust assets for the benefit of one or more beneficiaries. The trustee is named in the trust agreement. The trustmaker may also designate himself or herself as trustee and/or beneficiary.

TRUSTMAKER

The person who creates a trust. This person is also known as a trustor, grantor or settlor.

WILL

A document (sometimes also called a testament) in which someone sets out his or her instructions for settling his or her financial affairs after death – naming the persons to receive the assets, for example. The formal name for someone who writes a will is usually referred to as the *testator*. A will does not take effect until the death of the person who writes it.

NOTES